Pop!

A Play

Monica Hughes
Based on a story by Alison Hawes
Illustrated by Woody

RIGBY

The Characters

Kangaroo:
Look! I have some balloons.

Kangaroo:
The blue balloon is
for you.

Snake:
Thank you.
I like my blue balloon!

Kangaroo:
The little balloons are
for you.

Octopus:
Thank you.
I like my little balloons!

Hedgehog:

I like balloons, too.
Can I have a balloon?

Kangaroo:

Yes.
The big balloons are
for you.

Hedgehog:
Look at me!
Look at all **my** balloons!

Kangaroo:
Look out!
Look out!

Hedgehog:

Oh, no!

All my balloons went **pop**!

Octopus and Snake:

Oh, no!

All his balloons went **pop**!

POP
POP
POP
POP

Joey:
Look! You can have my balloon.

Hedgehog:
Thank you! Thank you!
Thank you!